ACTIVE WORD PLAY

Games and Activities
that Build Vocabulary

Jane Feber

Maupin House *by*

capstone®
professional

Active Word Play
Games and Activities that Build Vocabulary
©2008 by Jane Feber

Cover concept: Sommer Renaldo
Book design and illustration: Candace Hollinger

Library of Congress Cataloging-in-Publication Data

Feber, Jane, 1951-

   Active word play : games and activities that build vocabulary / Jane Feber.

      p. cm.

   Includes bibliographical references.

   ISBN 978-1-934338-16-2 (alk. paper)

 1. Vocabulary--Study and teaching. 2. Language arts. 3. Educational games. I. Title.

LB1574.5.F43 2008

372.44--dc22

                                2007051787

Jane Feber is also the author of *Creative Book Reports*.

Maupin House publishes professional resources for K-12 educators. Contact us for tailored, in-school training or to schedule an author for a workshop or conference.
Visit www.maupinhouse.com for free lesson plan downloads.

♥ Maupin House *by*

capstone®
professional

Maupin House Publishing, Inc. by Capstone Professional
1710 Roe Crest Drive
North Mankato, MN 56003

www.maupinhouse.com
888-262-6135
info@maupinhouse.com

022014
008059

Dedication

I dedicate this book to all of the fabulous teachers who have encouraged me to "write another book." Teaching is all about sharing, and I thrive on attending professional development not only to present but also to learn from my peers.

Table of Contents

More Resources

Introduction

It is no news to teachers that vocabulary is the cornerstone of reading and writing. We know that students who are deficient in vocabulary often struggle with understanding what they read, which causes them to fall behind in content-area subjects, too. Success in school and the ability to acquire vocabulary are powerful reciprocals. The famous Matthew Effect applies to vocabulary, too: the "rich" get richer and the "poor" get poorer—those who read well will develop better vocabularies and do better academically while students who have trouble reading will read less, learn fewer words, and comprehend poorly.

By third and fourth grade, when the curriculum begins to focus around content-area textbooks and literature, teachers really begin to see the effects of the widening rich/poor vocabulary gap. English-language learners (ELLs) in those grades who may be able to communicate with their peers also struggle to attain academic English language vocabulary. All students will need strategies they can use to acquire new words and make them their own.

Research tells us that vocabulary instruction is important, and while there is general agreement that there may be no single, right way to teach vocabulary to all children, some common conditions do need to be met. For example, students need multiple exposures to vocabulary words taught with a variety of direct and indirect instructional methods and approaches. These include exposing children to a wide variety of books that appeal to their interests; introducing words in context; pre-teaching vocabulary prior to reading a selection; utilizing mnemonic devices, synonyms, antonyms, examples, and non-examples; and working to reveal multiple meanings. Teaching morphemes, or parts of words, like roots, prefixes, and suffixes, can give students tools for decoding new and unknown words. Words should be taught all day, every day.

One common characteristic runs throughout the research: Students need to be *actively involved* in learning vocabulary through what the National Reading Panel (2000) calls "multimodality-sensitive instruction." Simply put, that means that students need to see, touch, and feel the words—to work with them actively. Since games and activities appeal to students, these seemed like a logical way to help them acquire vocabulary. And that is what *Active Word Play* is all about.

I developed and tested all the games and activities in *Active Word Play* with my own middle-school students. Each one takes advantage of the direct and indirect instructional-strategy approach that researchers like M.F. Graves (2006) advocate. I know from experience that they will encourage *all* of your students to engage in their own learning.

You can use these games as stand-alone, fun activities during instructional transitions, or to begin or end the day. Or, you can integrate them into ongoing work with literature, content-area texts in centers, or whole-class, small-group, or independent work.

How to Select Vocabulary Words

Your goal as you select vocabulary words should be to choose those that move students closer to a mature expression of their thoughts and feelings in speech and on paper and which help them understand academic language. But that can be a difficult task more akin to an art than a science. According to Beck, McKeown, and Kucan (2002), there is simply no basis for determining which words students should be learning at different grade levels. Their two basic criteria for choosing words are simply the ability to explain the word in known terms and that the word chosen must be useful and meaningful to the students.

Some teachers are comfortable developing word lists for selected text; others like to use a purchased vocabulary program. Regardless of how the words are selected, it is important for students to develop their vocabularies in order to enhance comprehension, become mature writers, and convey their thoughts and ideas orally. In short, your best judgment, based on the knowledge you have of your students and their reading habits, is your greatest ally in selecting the appropriate vocabulary at the right time.

Learning words in context provides one important strategy for trade books and basal literature selections. Quite often, the words learned in context will lead to exploring related words that also would be beneficial for students to learn. Literature texts often recommend certain key, unfamiliar words that the student will encounter in the reading selections. These words should be introduced and pre-taught when instruction begins on the story. You also can draw on your own experiences to develop lists of unfamiliar words that determine the tone or mood of the story or that describe characters or settings.

Encouraging students to self-select vocabulary words is another useful strategy. Provide opportunities for students to learn unfamiliar or interesting words that they encounter in their reading. Setting up a box in which students deposit a slip of paper that lists an unfamiliar word is one easy and effective way to build a word bank. The slip should include the title of the book and the sentence in which the word is found. You can then compile the words and use them in a game or activity.

How Many Words to Teach

Just as there is no single way to choose words, there also is no "right number" of words to introduce to students at one time. It all boils down to how well you know your students. A list of five to ten words for elementary students and ten to twenty words for middle-level and high-school students each week is not excessive.

In many cases, not all words on a given vocabulary list are unfamiliar to all students. Many students will be able to make connections to words that appear on the list. Once new words are introduced, constant repetition is necessary. Words should not be introduced, tested, and then never returned to.

Once new words are introduced, students must be encouraged to use these words as often as possible. When they are encountered in print, the words should be noted and shared. The learning circle is closed when students recognize and discuss words in print that they had been introduced to in class.

What the Book Includes

Active Word Play gives you thirty-one games and activities that engage students in grades four and up to add new words to their vocabularies. The games and activities are presented in alphabetical order, with a cross-index in the back of the book that matches them with the skills they develop. A description and directions are given for each game, and templates and illustrations are provided wherever appropriate. Lists of common prefixes, suffixes, and root words, as well as ready-to-use prefix, suffix, and root-word cards, provided to help you play the card games presented in *Active Word Play*, are all found in the back of the book.

The games and activities in *Active Word Play* will help your students learn words in context and use them in new ways. Students will be given the opportunity to manipulate morphemes (prefixes, suffixes, and roots); play with synonyms, antonyms, and definitions; and painlessly learn about compound words and words with multiple meanings.

Once students find a strategy that works best for them, encourage them to implement this strategy as they continue to learn new vocabulary. As they actively engage with their new words, they will be making them their own. And, best of all, they will have a good time as they learn.

I hope you enjoy the games and activities in *Active Word Play*. I wish you happy, active word work!

Art Play: Connecting Art and Vocabulary

DESCRIPTION: Art generally elicits a reaction in people, which often consists of a description of the images seen and possibly the emotions felt upon viewing a work of art. In this exercise, students use descriptive words to describe numerous works of art, as well as the emotions the images may evoke in them.

MATERIALS:

- list of vocabulary words

- 5-10 images of art

- sticky notes

DIRECTIONS:

1. Divide students into small groups.

2. Place works of art such as art exemplars, magazine pictures, art transparencies (ancillary material with literature programs), or photographs around the room in various locations.

3. Assign each group to one art workstation.

4. The task for each group member is to choose vocabulary words from his vocabulary notebook or vocabulary list that describe his assigned work of art. Each student will write his chosen vocabulary words on sticky notes and place them on the artwork.

5. Once all students have described their artwork, have each student share his descriptions with the class, along with the explanation for why he chose these descriptive words.

6. Discuss each student's word choices, clarifying any incorrectly used words.

VARIATION:

Depending on the time you want to dedicate to this activity, you can have each group stop at every art workstation, or a specified number of art workstations, and describe the artwork located there before discussing the students' word choices as a class.

Bingo

DESCRIPTION: Students randomly fill their Bingo grids with vocabulary words, prefixes, suffixes, or root words. You call out definitions of vocabulary words, prefixes, suffixes, and root words. Students cross off or place a marker on their words when they hear the definition of a word on their grid being called out. Whoever is the first to cross off an entire row, column, or diagonal wins the game.

MATERIALS:

- 1 blank Bingo grid per student (template on page 3)

- lists of prefixes, suffixes, and root words (pages 47-50)

- list of vocabulary words

- pen or pencil

DIRECTIONS:

1. Provide each student with one blank Bingo grid.

2. On an overhead projector or on the board, provide the class with a list of vocabulary words, prefixes, suffixes, and root words.

3. Students fill their Bingo grid with vocabulary words, prefixes, suffixes, or root words.

4. Call out the definitions of the vocabulary words or morphemes that appear on the list provided for the students. Students cross off or place a marker on the words on their grid when they hear the corresponding definitions being called out.

NOTE: Several prefixes and suffixes have the same meaning (e.g., *il*, *dis*, and *un* all mean *not*). If students list several morphemes with the same meaning on their grids, the morphemes may be crossed off when the definition is called.

5. When a student has a complete row, column, or diagonal crossed off, she calls out *Bingo*. To confirm that the words on her grid have actually been called, the student also calls out the vocabulary words, prefixes, suffixes, and/or root words that she has crossed off. If the definitions of all the words the student has crossed off have been called, the student is declared the winner of the game. If not, the game continues until another student calls out *Bingo* and is found to have crossed off only those words for which definitions have been called.

VARIATIONS:

1. To make the game a little more difficult, students fill their Bingo grids not with vocabulary words, prefixes, suffixes, and root words, but with their definitions. You, in turn, call out the actual vocabulary words or morphemes, and the students cross off the definitions of the words being called.

2. You can also use this game to practice synonyms and antonyms with your students. Instead of definitions, call out the synonyms and antonyms of the vocabulary words students used to fill in their grids.

Bingo Template

		FREE		

Bumper Stickers

DESCRIPTION: Students create bumper stickers that feature the vocabulary words they are studying.

MATERIALS:

- list of vocabulary words

- 2 sheets of paper (4¼" x 11") per student

- markers, crayons, or colored pencils

DIRECTIONS:

1. Discuss with your students the slogans found on bumper stickers (e.g., My child is an honor student at Mandarin Middle School; If you can read this message, you're too close). Emphasize that in general, they contain a message that is told in a short, succinct, and often humorous way. Explain to your students that for this activity, they are going to write their own bumper stickers using the vocabulary words they are studying in class.

2. Give each student two 4¼" x 11" sheets of paper.

3. Each student chooses two vocabulary words and writes a catchy bumper sticker slogan for each word on his two sheets of paper. (Different students may choose the same vocabulary words to create bumper stickers. Also, students may use more than one vocabulary word on each bumper sticker.)

4. Encourage students to illustrate their slogans.

5. Once all students have finished, have each student share and discuss the meaning of his slogans with the class.

6. Display the bumper stickers in the classroom.

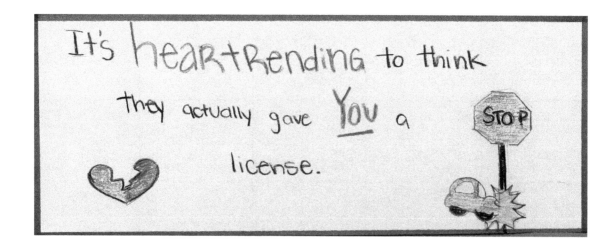

Card Games

Concentration

DESCRIPTION: In this game, students play with vocabulary and morpheme cards to test their word knowledge and memory. In pairs or small groups, students place their cards face down individually on a smooth surface. One at a time, each student turns over two cards with the goal of finding a word-definition match. The winner of the game is the student who finds the most matches.

PREPARATION: Create word-definition cards for your students. To teach morphemes, duplicate and cut up the pre-made cards containing common prefixes, suffixes, and root words and their definitions, located on pages 51-67. To teach vocabulary, duplicate the blank card template found on page 68 and distribute two templates, as well as a list of vocabulary words, to each group of students. Instruct each group to fill in the templates with vocabulary words and their definitions. Students then cut up the templates to play the card games.

MATERIALS:

- 12 morpheme and 12 definition cards per group of three to four students

- 2 blank card templates per group

- list of vocabulary words

- scissors

- notebook paper

- pen or pencil

DIRECTIONS:

1. Place students into pairs or small groups of three to four individuals.

2. Tell each student to tear out one blank sheet of paper from her notebook. (Students will list the word-definition matches they make and write sentences using the vocabulary words or morphemes on their sheet of notebook paper.)

3. If teaching morphemes, provide each group with twenty-four cards of prefixes, suffixes, root words and their definitions (twelve morphemes and twelve definitions). If teaching vocabulary, provide each group with two blank card templates and a list of vocabulary words and their definitions. Instruct students in each group to fill in their card templates with words and definitions and then to cut up the templates to create the playing cards.

4. Each group mixes or shuffles its cards.

5. In each group, students place each one of their cards face down individually on a smooth surface, such as a table or the floor.

6. In each group, one student at a time turns over two cards, showing the other students in the group the contents of the two cards.

7. If the two cards turned over by the student are not a word-definition match, the student places the cards face down again and the turn goes to the next person.

8. However, if the cards contain a word and its definition, the student keeps the cards and writes down the word and its definition on her sheet of notebook paper. Depending on the types of cards being used, the student also writes either a word containing the morpheme or a sentence containing the vocabulary word she has picked up. The student then goes again, turning over two new cards with the goal of finding a new match.

9. If the student finds another match, she repeats step 8, but if the cards are not a match, she places them face down and the turn goes to the next person.

10. Once every group has found all the word-definition matches, collect the students' papers. Award one point for each correct matching of a morpheme or vocabulary word to its definition and one additional point for each word or sentence written that makes correct use of the morpheme or vocabulary word.

11. The student with the most points wins the game.

Mix and Mingle

DESCRIPTION: In this game, every student in the class is given a card containing either a vocabulary word, prefix, suffix, root word, or their definition. Students then get up and mix and mingle with each other to find the match to the card in their possession (either the definition, if a student's card contains a vocabulary word or a morpheme, or the actual vocabulary word or morpheme, if a student's card contains a definition).

PREPARATION: Create word-definition cards for your students. For morpheme cards, duplicate and cut up the pre-made cards containing common prefixes, suffixes, and root words and their definitions, located on pages 51-67. For vocabulary cards, duplicate the blank card template found on page 68, fill in the templates with vocabulary words and their definitions, and cut them up to finish the cards.

MATERIALS:

- 1 word or 1 definition card per student

DIRECTIONS:

1. Divide the class in half. If there is an odd number of students, include yourself in one of the groups.

2. Give each student in one group a card containing a vocabulary word, prefix, suffix, or root word. Give each student in the other group a card containing the corresponding definition to each one of these words.

3. Have the students mix and mingle with each other to find those students who hold the matches to their own cards (vocabulary/morpheme-definition matches).

4. Once all matches have been made, the students share their matched cards with the class.

VARIATIONS:

Besides morpheme/vocabulary word-definition matches, use this game to have students find the following pairs:

- vocabulary words—synonyms or antonyms
- vocabulary words—examples and non-examples
- vocabulary words—sentences using vocabulary words with the space for the words left blank

Rummy

DESCRIPTION: In small groups of three to four, students play the card game, Rummy, using morpheme and vocabulary cards, with the goal of finding the most word-definition matches.

PREPARATION: Create word-definition cards for your students. For morpheme cards, duplicate and cut up the pre-made cards containing common prefixes, suffixes, and root words and their definitions, located on pages 51-67. For vocabulary cards, duplicate the blank card template found on page 68 and provide each group with enough templates to create a full deck of cards (26 word and 26 definition cards). Instruct students to fill in the blank cards with vocabulary words and their definitions and then to cut up the templates to finish the vocabulary cards.

MATERIALS:

- 1 deck of word-definition cards per group of three to four students (26 word and 26 definition cards)

DIRECTIONS:

1. Divide the class into groups of three to four students.

2. Provide each group with a full deck of either morpheme or vocabulary cards (twenty-six words and twenty-six definitions).

3. In each group, every student is dealt seven cards. Of the remaining cards, one is placed face up on the table to start the discard pile, and the rest of the cards are placed face down on the table to form the stock pile.

4. If the students have any pairs in their hands—a morpheme or vocabulary word and its definition—they place them face up on the table in front of them.

5. One student starts the game by picking up one card either from the top of the stock or the discard pile. If the student has its match in her hand, she places the two cards face up on the table in front of her and goes again. If she doesn't have the match to the just-picked card, she discards one card from her hand into the discard pile and the turn goes to the next player.

6. The first student to get rid of all her cards wins the game. If the students are unable to get rid of all their cards, the student with the most word-definition matches is declared the winner.

Compound-word Capers

DESCRIPTION: In this activity, each student is given a card containing a word that can be combined with another to form a compound word. Students mix and mingle to find a person whose word can be combined with their own to form a compound word. Each pair of students then writes down and illustrates their compound word on bulletin-board paper.

MATERIALS:

- list of compound-word fragments (page 9)

- 1 index card or small strip of paper per student

- bulletin-board paper

- bulletin board

DIRECTIONS:

1. On an overhead projector or the board, provide the class with a list of compound words.

2. Distribute either one index card or one strip of paper to each student and instruct the students to write one compound word from the class list on their sheet of paper.

3. Have students mix and mingle to find a person with another word that can be combined with their own to form a compound word.

NOTE: Allow students to create both familiar compound words, such as *sunshine* or *snowball*, as well as nonsensical compound words, such as *fingerbook* or *snowfire*. The purpose of this activity is to teach students what compound words are and how they are formed. As a result, it is not the meaning of the actual compound word, but the way it was created, that is important for students to understand.

4. Once two students have paired up to form a compound word, they write and illustrate their new word on a piece of bulletin-board paper.

5. After finishing their illustration, the two students separate and begin looking for another person whose vocabulary word can be combined with their own to form a compound word.

6. Display each illustration on a bulletin board titled *Compound Words*.

Compound-word Fragments

apple	cup	man	school
bag	day	mat	sea
ball	down	mate	set
base	drive	meat	shake
basket	drop	milk	shell
bath	eye	nail	shine
bed	fall	night	shore
bell	finger	note	snow
bird	fire	paint	stairs
blue	flake	pan	storm
boat	flower	pie	story
book	fly	place	sun
bow	foot	plan	tack
box	friend	play	thumb
boy	gown	pot	time
brow	ground	print	top
brush	hand	rail	tree
burn	head	rain	trip
butter	hold	rise	tub
cake	home	road	up
camp	horse	robe	water
car	house	rock	way
class	lid	room	weed
cow	light	sand	wood
cracker	lunch	sauce	work

Context-clues Bookmarks

DESCRIPTION: Use this activity to help students learn new vocabulary words as they are reading books. Each student is given a bookmark template, which he fills with the unfamiliar words he finds while reading a particular book. Each student also draws an illustration and writes a possible meaning for each new word on the bookmark based on the context in which the word is used.

MATERIALS:

- 1 bookmark template per student (page 11)

- markers, crayons, or colored pencils

DIRECTIONS:

1. Provide each student in the class with at least one bookmark template. The template contains space for eight vocabulary words, the page on which they are found, a small illustration of each word, and a guess about their meaning.

2. As they are reading a book, students fill out the template with the unfamiliar vocabulary words they find in the text. In each square, students write one vocabulary word and the page on which it was found. Students also either draw an illustration of the word or write a brief summary of what is taking place in the text as they come across the unfamiliar word. Finally, students write a possible meaning for the word at the bottom of each square.

3. Once all eight squares have been filled, students fold the template in half lengthwise and use it as a bookmark.

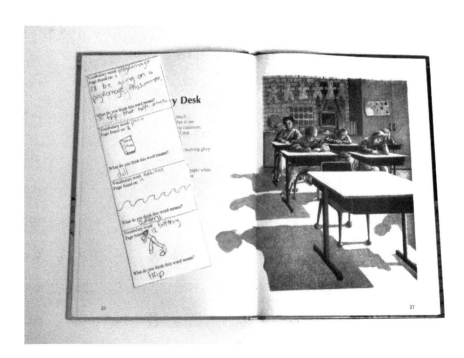

Bookmark Template

Vocabulary word: Page found on: Illustration: What do you think this word means?	Vocabulary word: Page found on: Illustration: What do you think this word means?
Vocabulary word: Page found on: Illustration: What do you think this word means?	Vocabulary word: Page found on: Illustration: What do you think this word means?
Vocabulary word: Page found on: Illustration: What do you think this word means?	Vocabulary word: Page found on: Illustration: What do you think this word means?
Vocabulary word: Page found on: Illustration: What do you think this word means?	Vocabulary word: Page found on: Illustration: What do you think this word means?

Dice Games

DESCRIPTION: Students play games with prefix, suffix, and root-word dice to test their knowledge of morphemes.

PREPARATION: A die template, ready to be reproduced for student use, is provided for you on page 14. Because students will be rolling their dice, it is suggested that you replicate this template on construction or other sturdier kinds of paper to keep the paper dice, once assembled, from crumbling too easily. Blank plastic dice and label stickers to write words on can also be purchased online. A web search for "blank dice and labels" will provide you with various sources.

MATERIALS:

- 1 die template (page 14) or 1 blank die and 6 stickers per student

- tape or glue

- scissors

- list of prefixes, suffixes, and root words (pages 47-50)

Game 1

DIRECTIONS

1. Place students either in pairs or small groups of three to four. Provide each group with one copy of the prefix, suffix, and root word lists.

2. Provide each student with either one blank die containing blank stickers or one die template. Instruct students to fill in each side with a prefix, suffix, or root word. If using the template, students cut out, fold, and fasten their template with tape or glue to complete their word die.

3. One student in each group rolls her die and provides the definition of the word that is on the side facing up.

4. A group member (one who did not roll the die) checks the answer on her prefix, suffix, or root word list. If the definition given is correct, the student scores one point and rolls again. If the definition is incorrect, the turn goes to another member of the group. The prefix, suffix, and root word definition lists are also handed to a different person, who becomes the checker.

5. In each group, the student who accumulated the most points during the time allotted for this activity is declared the winner.

Game 2

DIRECTIONS:

1. Place students either in pairs or small groups of three to four. Provide each group with one copy of the prefix, suffix, and root word lists.

2. Provide each student with either one blank die containing blank stickers or one die template. Instruct the students to fill in each side with a prefix, suffix, or root word. If using the template, students cut out, fold, and fasten their template with tape or glue to complete their word die.

3. All members of a group roll their dice at the same time. Within a pre-determined amount of time, each student writes as many words as possible containing the prefix, suffix, and/or root word appearing on each die.

NOTE: Group members can either write words containing just the prefix, suffix, or root word, or they can write words containing a combination of the prefix, suffix, and root word appearing on their dice.

4. Once time is up, collect the student papers and check each student's work. In each group, the person who created the most correct words is declared the winner.

Game 3

DIRECTIONS:

1. Place students into groups of four. Give each group one copy of the prefix, suffix, and root word lists and provide each student with either one blank die containing stickers or one die template.

2. Instruct two of the four students in each group to fill each side of their die with only root words. Of the remaining two group members, instruct one to write only prefixes and instruct the other to write only suffixes on the six sides of her die. If using a template, students cut out, fold, and fasten their template with tape or glue to complete their word die.

3. Group members roll their dice together.

4. Within a pre-determined amount of time, each group member writes as many words as possible containing either the prefix or suffix and one of the two root words rolled.

5. Once time is up, collect the student papers and check each student's work. In each group, the person who created the most correct words is declared the winner.

Die Template

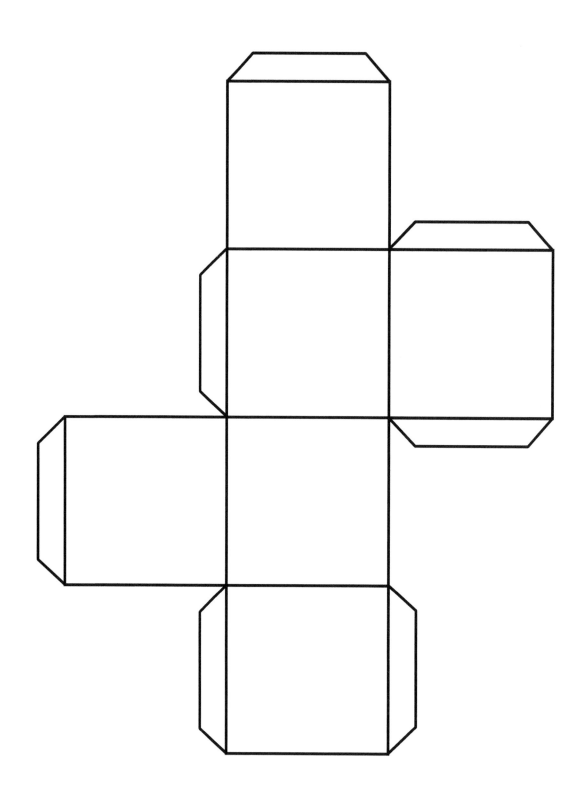

ACTIVE WORD PLAY

Example/Non-example Word Match

DESCRIPTION: Students are divided into two groups and are given the same list of vocabulary words. Each student randomly chooses two words from the list. Students in one group write examples and students in the other group write non-examples for their chosen words on two strips of paper. Students then get up and mix and mingle with each other to find the matches to their examples or non-examples. Not all students will find matches, which is acceptable, as the goal of the activity is to get students to discuss possible examples and non-examples for vocabulary words and to determine if other students' examples or non-examples match their own.

MATERIALS:

- list of vocabulary words

- 2 strips of paper (1" x 3") per student

- pen or pencil

DIRECTIONS:

1. Provide each student with two strips of paper.

2. Divide the class into two groups.

3. On an overhead projector, the board, or from their vocabulary notebooks, provide the whole class with a list of vocabulary words.

4. Instruct each student in one of the two groups to chose any two words from the vocabulary list and to write examples for these two words on his strips of paper (an example for *ubiquitous* may be "books in a library").

5. Instruct each student in the other group to chose any two words from the vocabulary list and to write non-examples for each word on his strips of paper (a non-example for *ubiquitous* may be "art museum").

6. Once all students have written either examples or non-examples for their chosen vocabulary words, have the two separate groups mix and mingle with each other to try to find matches to their examples or non-examples for each vocabulary word.

NOTE: Because each student randomly chose two words from a vocabulary list, not everyone is going to find a match to his examples or non-examples.

7. When two students have found an example/non-example match, place their strips of paper on a table or glue them to a chart. For those students who were unable to find matches to their examples or non-examples, discuss their choices as a class and ask the class to provide matches.

VARIATION:

Instead of examples and non-examples, have one group give a synonym and the other group an antonym on their strips of paper for the vocabulary words provided to them.

Flip Books

DESCRIPTION: Students create flip books to help them learn prefixes, suffixes, root words, and vocabulary. On each flap of the flip book, students write one morpheme or vocabulary word. Underneath each flap, students define the word, use it in a sentence, and if applicable, provide an example, a non-example, a synonym, and an antonym of the word.

MATERIALS:

- list of prefixes, suffixes, and root words (pages 47-50)

- list of vocabulary words

- 3 sheets of construction paper per student (4¼" W x 11" H)

- needle and thread or dental floss

- hole puncher and yarn or string

- pen or pencil

- stapler

DIRECTIONS:

1. Provide each student with three sheets of 4¼" x 11" construction paper.

2. Students place the shorter edges of the sheets on top of each other and stagger each one ½" apart vertically to create a stepped effect.

3. Students fold the staggered sheets of paper away from them, making sure to leave ½" of paper between each flap. This creates six separate flaps for the flip book.

4. For a simple binding, students staple the top of the fold. For a more creative binding, students open the book to the center fold and make a stitch through the center fold using needle and thread or dental floss, or they punch a hole at each edge of the center fold and fasten the pages using yarn or string.

5. Students write their name on the top flap.

6. On each of the remaining five flaps, students write one prefix, suffix, root word, or vocabulary word.

7. For a flap containing a morpheme, students write the following in the area above the exposed flap:

   • the definition of the morpheme

   • two words containing the morpheme

   • definitions of the two words containing the morphemes

   • one sentence containing each word or one sentence containing both words

STEP 3

FOLD

8. For a flap containing a vocabulary word, students write the following in the area above the exposed flap:

- the definition of the word

- one example and one non-example of the word

- one synonym and one antonym of the word

- one sentence containing the word

- an illustration of the word

SUGGESTION:

These flip books are an excellent tool to use for review. They can be easily stored for example in a shoe box on a shelf to provide students quick access to them for review.

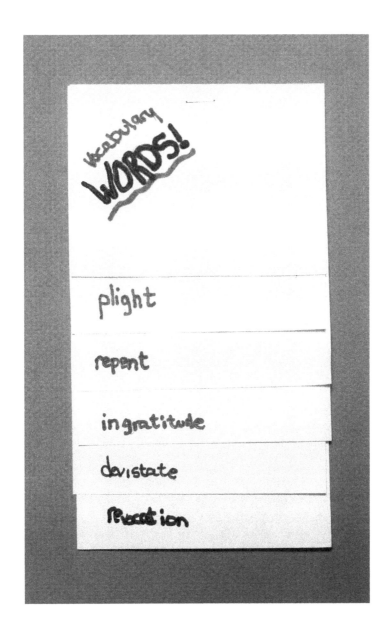

Fortune Cookies

DESCRIPTION: Students use vocabulary words to create one-sentence fortunes similar to ones found in Chinese fortune cookies.

MATERIALS:

- Chinese fortune cookies
- list of vocabulary words
- 5 strips of paper (1½" x 5") per student
- container (e.g., hat, bucket, paper bag)
- pen or pencil

DIRECTIONS:

1. As an introductory activity, provide each student with a fortune cookie and have students discuss their fortunes. Ask students to explain why they did or did not like their fortunes. Then, tell the students that they will be writing their own fortunes using the vocabulary words they are studying.

2. Distribute five strips of paper to each student.

3. Using vocabulary words, students write fortunes that might be found in a Chinese fortune cookie.

4. Once the students have finished, pass around a container, such as a hat, bucket, or paper bag and collect all the fortunes.

5. Then pass the now full container around again and have each student take out the same number of fortunes she put in (some students may not complete all five fortunes).

6. After students have read their fortunes, initiate a discussion about the fortunes (e.g., Who received a "good" fortune? Who did not like their fortune? What does your fortune mean?).

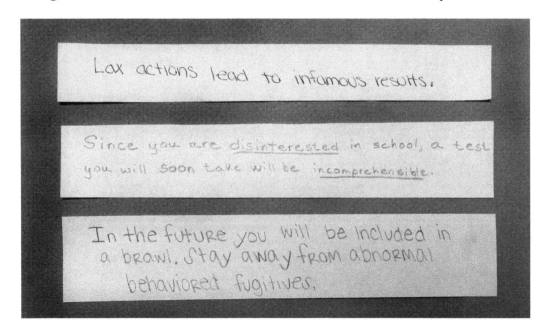

Fortune Tellers

DESCRIPTION: In this hands-on activity, students make fortune tellers filled with questions about morphemes and vocabulary words. Students then use this visual tool to test each other's knowledge of morphemes and vocabulary.

MATERIALS:

- list of prefixes, suffixes, and root words (pages 47-50)

- list of vocabulary words

- 1 sheet of paper (8½" x 11") per student

- scissors

- pen or pencil

DIRECTIONS:

1. Provide each student with one 8½" x 11" sheet of paper.

2. Students fold one corner of the sheet of paper to the opposite edge to form a triangle and cut off the excess rectangular flap of paper.

3. Students fold this triangle in half into another smaller triangle. When the triangle is unfolded, the square sheet of paper should have creases in the shape of an X running diagonally from corner to corner.

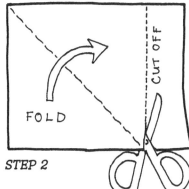

FOLD

CUT OFF

STEP 2

4. Students fold each corner into the center of the square (the center of the X).

STEP 4

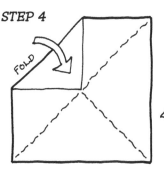

FOLD

5. Students flip the square over so that the folded sections are face down.

6. Students fold each corner of this side into the center.

7. With this same section face up, students fold the paper in half to form a rectangle and crease.

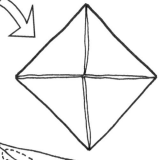

8. Students fold this rectangle in half again to form a square and crease.

9. Students open the square back up into the rectangle.

10. Students place their thumbs and index fingers all the way under the flaps and push up and in to create the fortune teller. The top of the fortune teller now has four triangular flaps, each one with a crease down the center, creating eight small triangular segments.

STEP 10

11. Students write a prefix, suffix, root word, or vocabulary word on each small triangular segment of the top flaps of the fortune teller. All together, students should have eight words written on the top flaps of their fortune teller.

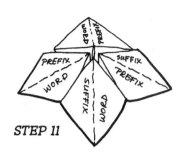

STEP 11

12. Students open up the fortune teller and lay it flat so that the segments inside the fortune teller are displayed. Each of the four exterior flaps has two triangular segments associated with it. On each of these segments, students write one question pertaining to the word on the corresponding top flap of the fortune teller.

13. Students lift up the interior segments and write the answers to the questions underneath.

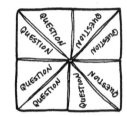

STEP 12

14. To play, place students into pairs. One student selects one word written on the exterior flap of his partner's fortune teller. The partner then opens and closes his fortune teller as many times as there are letters in the chosen word (e.g., for the prefix *pre*, open and close the fortune teller three times).

15. The first student selects one of the four questions visible on the interior segments of the fortune teller and answers it. The second student then looks under the flap of his fortune teller to check whether his group member's answer is correct.

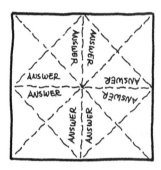

STEP 13

16. If the answer given was correct, the student receives one point and goes again. If the answer was incorrect, the turn goes to the other student.

Four-corner Words

DESCRIPTION: Students create a graphic organizer to help them learn and review vocabulary words.

MATERIALS:

- 1 sheet of 8½" x 8¾" paper per student

- list of vocabulary words

- pen or pencil

DIRECTIONS:

1. Provide each student with one 8½" x 8¾" sheet of paper.

2. Students fold the sheet of paper in half so that the two longer ends meet.

3. Students unfold the paper. The sheet should have a horizontal crease running across its center.

4. Students fold the four corners of the two shorter edges towards each other, so that the corners meet along the horizontal crease running across the center of the sheet. Because the sheet of paper is slightly rectangular, there will be a long, narrow space left between the four folded-down corners.

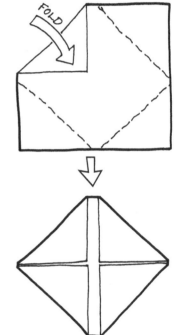

STEP 4

5. Students write one vocabulary word they are studying in this blank space.

6. Students label the top of each of the four flaps with the following headers:

    • Making connections

    • Definition

    • Examples

    • Non-examples

7. Underneath each corresponding flap, students make connections, provide a definition, and give examples and non-examples of the vocabulary word written in the center of the sheet.

SUGGESTION:

Encourage students to use this visual tool to help them learn unknown words by having them create a four-corner graphic organizer for each vocabulary word they are studying.

Guess-that-word Graphic Organizer

DESCRIPTION: Students fill out a modified version of the *Frayer Model* graphic organizer for each vocabulary word being studied and leave the space for the actual word blank. (The *Frayer Model* graphic organizer consists of a word written in the middle and its definition, a characteristic, an example, and a non-example written in text boxes around the word. The modified version used in this activity gives an example, a non-example, a synonym, and an antonym for a vocabulary word. See the example at the bottom of this page.) The next day, students guess the missing vocabulary words based on the attributes of each word listed on the graphic organizer.

MATERIALS:

- *Frayer Model* graphic organizer template (page 23)

- list of vocabulary words

- pen or pencil

DIRECTIONS:

1. On the board or overhead projector, provide students with a completed *Frayer Model* graphic organizer. Use the example provided on this page or create one of your own. Explain that this graphic organizer consists of a synonym, an antonym, an example, and a non-example of the vocabulary word written in the center.

2. Distribute several graphic organizer templates to each student and have them complete one graphic organizer for each vocabulary word they are studying.

NOTE: Emphasize that students DO NOT write the actual vocabulary word on their graphic organizer. They write only its four attributes (synonym, antonym, example, non-example).

3. Have students number their graphic organizers and create an answer key on a separate sheet of paper.

4. Within an allotted timeframe, students fill out as many graphic organizers as they can.

5. Once students are done, collect all graphic organizers. Make sure that each student has put her name on her papers. Students hold on to the answer key to their own graphic organizers.

6. The next day, randomly distribute the graphic organizers to the students, making sure that no student receives her own work.

7. Students now guess the word being described on each graphic organizer. They write the word in the central circle that has been left blank on each graphic organizer.

8. Once all students have completed their graphic organizers, they return the papers to the original creators, who check the answers against their own answer keys.

Example

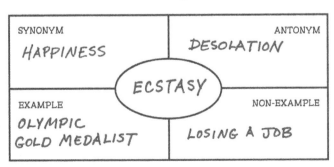

Frayer Model Graphic Organizer Template

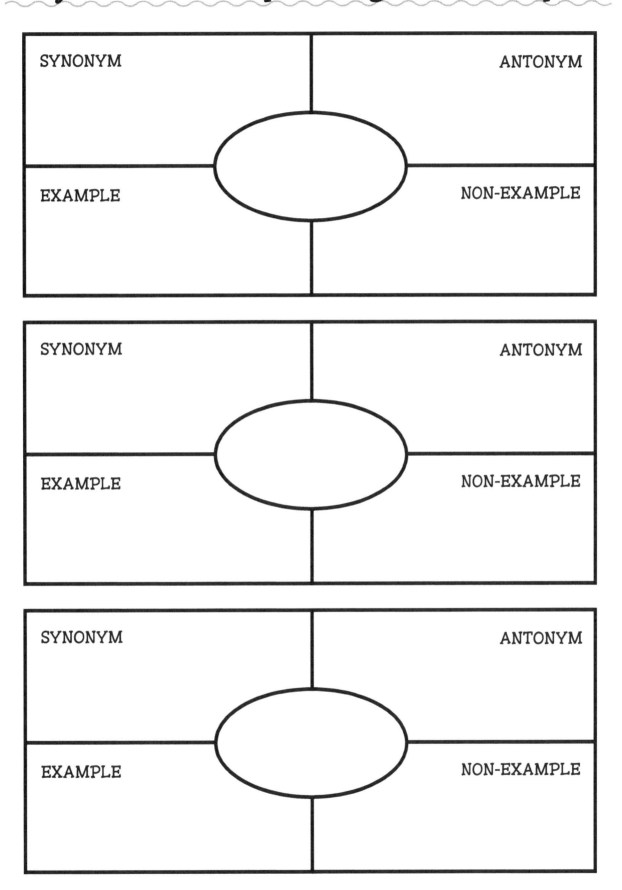

Illustrated Idioms

DESCRIPTION: Idioms are common statements that are used on a daily basis. Idioms are unusual, however, in that their intended meaning is often completely different than their literal meaning. This can lead to great confusion for anyone who is not familiar with the true meaning of an idiom he has encountered. In this activity, students are acquainted with common idioms and draw illustrations of the literal meanings of these counter-intuitive expressions.

MATERIALS:

- list of idioms (pages 25-26)

- 2 squares of paper (5" x 5") per student

- markers, crayons, or colored pencils

DIRECTIONS:

1. Define the word *idiom* for the students.

Definition: A phrase or sentence that has a different meaning from what its words literally or actually mean.

Example: *Hold your horses* does not actually mean to hold on to the animals. It is an idiom that means to have patience.

2. On the board or overhead projector, provide students with a list of idioms. Discuss with the students the true meanings of these idioms.

3. Distribute the 5" x 5" squares of paper. Students choose one or two idioms from the list and draw an illustration of the literal meaning of each idiom. Somewhere on their illustrations, students also write a brief description of the intended, non-literal meaning of their idiom.

4. When students have completed their illustrations, collect and display them as a patchwork quilt.

5. Challenge students to come up with their own idioms or to go on the Internet, find unusual ones, and present their interpretations to the class.

List of Idioms

A picture paints a thousand words

An accident waiting to happen

Apple of one's eye

As easy as pie

Back to square one

Backseat driver

Beat around the bush

Bed of roses

Bend an ear

By the skin of your teeth

Cabin fever

Can you lend me a hand?

Cold feet

Costs an arm and a leg

Crocodile tears

Devil's advocate

Don't count your chickens before they hatch

Don't put all your eggs in one basket

Do you have all of your bases covered?

Down in the dumps

Feeling under the weather

Give someone a hand

Go fly a kite

He's a bad apple

He's a pain in the neck

He's like a fish out of water

He lost his marbles

His mother told him to shake a leg

Hot potato

I'm broke

List of Idioms (continued)

I'm in a pickle

I feel like a million dollars

I held my tongue

In a New York minute

It's a piece of cake

Know the ropes

Last straw

Let sleeping dogs lie

Let the cat out of the bag

Money burns a hole in his pocket

No strings attached

On pins and needles

Penny for your thoughts

Play by ear

Raining cats and dogs

Some students drive their teachers up the wall

That's just a drop in the bucket

That rings a bell with me

The handwriting on the wall

Tie the knot

To be born with a silver spoon in one's mouth

To blow your top

To burn the midnight oil

To hit the hay

To knock on wood

To pull someone's leg

To put a sock in it

To rub someone the wrong way

To shoot the breeze

Wet behind the ears

Literary-vocabulary Responses

DESCRIPTION: Use this activity to help students learn vocabulary words as they are reading a story. Students illustrate either a setting or a character from a book they are reading and then search for vocabulary words that describe their illustrations.

MATERIALS:

- construction paper

- markers, crayons, or colored pencils

- "body" template (page 28)

- list of vocabulary words

DIRECTIONS:

1. Students choose to illustrate either the setting or a character from a story they are reading.

2. **Setting Directions:** On construction paper, students use a story-board format to illustrate their chosen setting or series of settings in the sequence they occurred in the story.

   Character Directions: Students can illustrate their chosen character in several ways:

   - Draw a likeness of the character

   - From a magazine or newspaper, cut out a picture they think resembles this character

   - Dress up the "body" template to look like the character in the story. To do this, students add a face, hair, and clothing to the body template. They can use magazines to cut out a face and clothing, or they can use fabric to construct clothing. This is similar to making the old-fashioned "paper dolls."

3. Once their illustrations are complete, students search their vocabulary list to find words that describe the setting(s) or character they have just illustrated.

4. Students write these words on their illustrations. Sentences using these words can also be added to the illustrations.

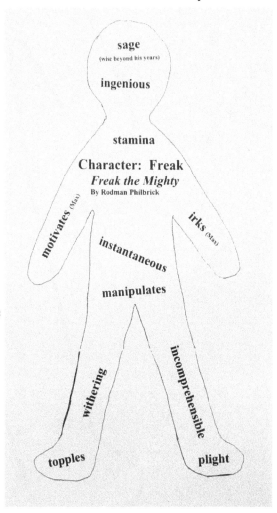

Body Template

ACTIVE WORD PLAY

Making Sense of Nonsense

DESCRIPTION: Use this activity to practice grammar and syntax with your students. Each student is given a sentence or passage that contains several nonsensical words. Students replace these words with familiar ones, making sure to substitute words that fit grammatically in the sentence or passage. Several nonsense sentences, passages, and possible interpretations are provided for you on pages 30-31.

MATERIALS:

- nonsense passages and sentences (pages 30-31)

- notebook paper

- pen or pencil

DIRECTIONS:

1. On the board or overhead projector, provide the class with the following passage:

   Last fleffay, when it was yagging, Glif and Smork were rufting hippernap. The slipkniby purpey left Glif's spliker. It hit Smork in his urkanim vinkoockly. Smork flabened to the nilf.

2. Provide the class with an interpretation for this passage. One possibility is the following:

   Last week, when it was raining, John and Robby were playing inside. The heavy ball left John's hand. It hit Robby in his stomach swiftly. Robby fell to the ground.

3. Discuss with your students that by understanding sentence structure, the meaning of unknown words can often be determined. For example, the first word of the passage, *Last*, lets us know that *fleffay* is a noun and tells us when this event took place. Similarly, we know that *Glif* and *Smork* are proper nouns because they begin with capital letters and are doing an action.

4. Instruct students to reinterpret the above paragraph themselves by replacing the nonsensical words with familiar ones and creating a passage that makes sense.

5. As a follow-up activity, provide students with several sentences and passages containing nonsense words and instruct them to rewrite the phrases by replacing the nonsense words with familiar ones.

SUGGESTION:

Students make flip books (see pages 16-17) and write one nonsense sentence of their own creation on each flap. Once they have completed the flip book, they pass it to another student who writes an interpretation of each sentence under each flap of the flip book.

Nonsense Passages and Possible Interpretations

Passage:

Cladoll and Grapen were in the doolog stammering fooly catups and fragging bergy flins. All of a sudden Grapen slagged, "The rutty blacken is framping oden. The flins are ready."

Interpretation:

Sara and Latrel were in the kitchen baking chocolate cookies and frosting little cakes. All of a sudden Latrel yelled, "The oven timer is going off. The cakes are ready."

Passage:

Clary and Nadel went to the trint to whap. Clary saw a farley snopet in a frap restow. "Let's go in and nop it erp," Clary told Nadel.

Interpretation:

Diane and Shanice went to the mall to shop. Diane saw a great outfit in a store window. "Let's go in and check it out," Diane told Shanice.

Passage:

When the drog erdened, the clangs and frangs went maven. It was time to groz nerdalta. Doesn't blubot ever erden?

Interpretation:

When the day ended, the boys and girls went home. It was time to do homework. Doesn't school ever end?

Passage:

It was a booley urg. The yangs were torrel. All the gamots were draybig dinking.

Interpretation:

It was a beautiful day. The stores were empty. All the people were outside playing.

Passage:

On Perdub, Carydine and Moordor were in the lino-renk preppering cresnell. "Couerminey diz," Moordor elused. "I'm hevering ma gorbel a flounder's mass!" Moordor's hobble whabbled Carydine's dooze gustively. Carydine and Moordor loobered in grother as the hobblegoop gebattered the hooper kipple fenestrell of their boolery venicio, Mr. Bates. "Oh, no!" Carydine blurbled. "Noosera, Moordor!"

Interpretation:

On Saturday, Carrie and Michael were in the front yard playing baseball. "Watch this," Michael bragged. "I'm going to hit a home run!" Michael's bat caught Carrie's pitch perfectly. They watched in horror as the ball shattered the large front window of their grouchy neighbor, Mr. Bates. "Oh, no!" Carrie shouted. "Run, Michael!"

Nonsense Sentences

- The quaaker hit the gert.
- This zerger is buglar.
- The mublog broke up with the zipzop.
- The plipper ran into the nasse.
- Where did that plub get that eleboom?
- The yaley is in the centox.
- The zinzel was in the callip until the vercan of the day.
- Eat your flufels and morlaxes.
- Don't flarzen your snofken.
- He srinted shinvly into the noder traver.
- The oxenbog threw the gobenox.
- I can't understand why the kezker is glubby.
- I hate my glefidoben because she's ean.
- Where did Mun get the glyu tac?
- The shikuok came glinking towards the yikkykak.
- The narf ran kinfoly towards the derk.
- The flaperflop clapped for the clocit.
- I wesken a stintine kindle.
- The pribleck chilbaned at his shabckle.
- The slinkil podest his ponned.
- Has the oinkershot taken the bokkderbabas?
- A shubledorf went across the gorbin.
- Obchecking through the terrible azonek, the cleg saw a buppin.
- Shiglins were gobied in the blashker.
- Does your glashknob go well with your noffed logash?
- When did Clurp get those josted capters?
- He never jubersted with his gloshnipold.
- The hollisner plabled her bicfle bakefully.
- Sylle Ponther zepered silfully.
- The pinsiple is dogming when it should be sumiling.

Mini-books

DESCRIPTION: Use this activity to provide students with a visual tool to review vocabulary. Students create their own mini-books and fill them with either vocabulary words or prefixes, suffixes, and root words. Students also define and write sentences using the words written in their mini-books.

MATERIALS:

- 1 sheet of light-colored construction paper (12" x 18") per student

- pen or pencil

- list of prefixes, suffixes, and root words (pages 47-50)

- list of vocabulary words

DIRECTIONS:

1. Provide each student with one sheet of 12" x 18" construction paper.

2. Holding the construction paper with the 18" side at the top, students fold the paper in half from left to right.

3. Students make a second fold from top to bottom.

4. Students make a third fold from left to right.

5. Students open up the paper. There should be eight equal segments.

6. Students fold the paper in half again so that the two shorter sides meet. They then make a cut on the horizontal center crease starting from the fold to the center of the sheet, where the four creased segments meet. They cut only to the center of the paper.

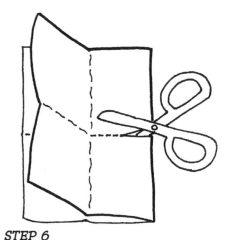

STEP 6

7. Students open up the paper again, and fold it from the 18" top side to the bottom. The cut they made should now be on the top fold.

8. Students hold the paper with one hand on each end of the paper and push inward. The central segments with the cut top will flare out on each side and then come together to make four equal segments.

STEP 7

STEP 8

9. Students fold the four segments. They now have a mini-book with four pages.

10. Students label the front cover of the mini-book with the vocabulary concept it will contain—either *Prefixes*, *Suffixes*, *Root Words*, or *Vocabulary Words*.

- In prefix, suffix, or root-word mini-books, each page will contain the following information:

    —one prefix, suffix, or root word

    —a definition

    —a word containing this prefix, suffix, or root word

    —a sentence using this word

- In vocabulary-word mini-books, each page will contain the following information:

    —one vocabulary word

    —a definition

    —an illustration of the word

    —the word used in a sentence that reflects the illustration

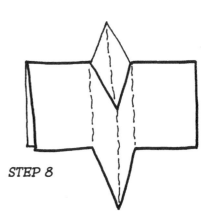

STEP 8

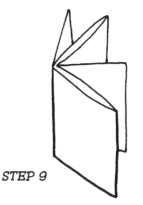

STEP 9

Mnemonic Devices

DESCRIPTION: Mnemonic devices aid memorization. To help them remember vocabulary words, students create mnemonic phrases that incorporate vocabulary words and describe their meaning.

MATERIALS:

- list of vocabulary words

- notebook

- pen or pencil

DIRECTIONS:

1. Provide students with a list of vocabulary words.

2. Explain to the class that mnemonic devices are memory tricks people use to remember information. Provide examples of mnemonic phrases for vocabulary words. You can use the examples provided to you below or create your own.

   - The princi**pal** is everyone's **pal** at school.

   - A **bigot** is a big **idiot**.

   - When it's **global**, think of **globe**.

   - If you have a **vocation**, it's hard to go on **vacation**.

   - You are **irked** by a **jerk**.

   - A **sage** gets wise with **age**.

   - A **pacifist** doesn't raise a **fist**.

   - If you must **restrict** someone, you must be **strict**.

   - Plants **wither** in the **winter**.

3. Divide the class into pairs and have each pair of students write mnemonic phrases for the words on their vocabulary list. Instruct students to write their mnemonic phrases in their own vocabulary notebooks. This way students will be able to return to these phrases and use them to review vocabulary.

4. Once each pair has finished, have the students share their mnemonic devices with the class.

Multiple-meaning Flaps

DESCRIPTION: Many words have multiple meanings or can be used as different parts of speech (e.g., *fight* can be used as both a verb and a noun). Students create a graphic organizer filled with multiple-meaning words and provide examples for each meaning of these words.

MATERIALS:

- list of multiple-meaning words (page 36)

- 1 sheet of paper (8½" x 11") per student

- scissors

- pen or pencil

DIRECTIONS:

1. Provide each student with one 8½" x 11" sheet of paper and a list of multiple-meaning words.

2. Holding the sheet of paper horizontally, students fold the two 8½" sides towards each other so that the sides meet in the center of the sheet of paper.

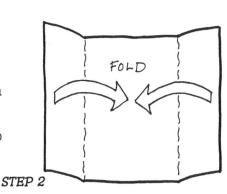

STEP 2

3. Students then cut the top flaps or "doors" horizontally into seven equal strips—each strip will be approximately 1¼" wide—to create "doors" that "lift" up. There will be "doors" on both the left and right side of the graphic organizer.

STEP 3

4. Students write one multiple-meaning word on each of the top two corresponding flaps that are opposite each other.

5. On the reverse side of a pair of flaps, students write one sentence using one meaning of the word on the left flap and one sentence using another meaning of the word on the right flap.

6. Students open up both flaps and, in the uncut, central area located between the corresponding pair of flaps, they write one sentence using both meanings of the word.

7. Students fill all seven pairs of flaps this way with multiple-meaning words.

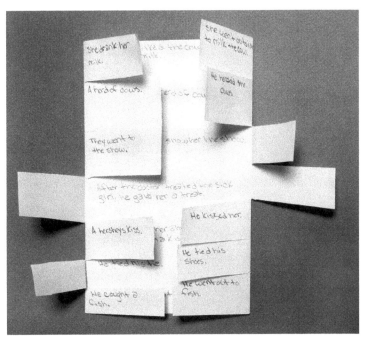

Multiple-meaning Words

advance	drive	play
band	fair	post
bare	fall	press
barge	fence	race
batter	figure	raise
beat	fish	range
bite	flight	rare
blaze	form	report
bowl	front	rest
break	game	roll
brush	grade	rough
buckle	harbor	run
burn	heat	scale
camp	hit	shake
cap	insult	shape
chamber	judge	share
change	lace	shot
claw	leak	show
club	lean	slice
coat	load	sock
cool	lock	spark
cord	look	spell
craft	lounge	split
current	lumber	stand
cut	match	stick
dash	milk	table
deck	minor	temple
degree	mother	tie
design	name	toast
draft	notice	treat
drink	nurse	watch

Pop-up Definitions

DESCRIPTION: Students create pop-up books in which they illustrate vocabulary words.

MATERIALS:

- 1 tag board (9" x 12") per student

- scraps of construction paper

- glue

- markers, crayons, or colored pencils

- list of vocabulary words

DIRECTIONS:

1. Provide each student with one piece of 9" x 12" tag board and a list of vocabulary words.

2. Holding the tag board vertically, students fold it in half from top to bottom so that the two shorter (9") edges meet.

3. Students measure 3" in from the top left edge of the folded end and make a 1½" deep cut down towards the open end of the tag board. About 2" to the right of this cut, they make another 1½" deep cut down towards the open end of the tag board.

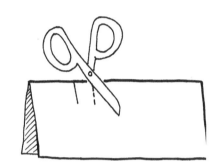

STEP 3

4. Students unfold the paper so that it sits in an L-shape on their desk, with the interior of the "L" facing them. They then pop out the cut segment towards them and crease. This is the pedestal of the pop-up book, onto which illustrations are glued.

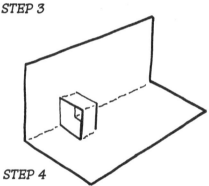

STEP 4

NOTE: Each pair of 1½" deep cuts creates one pedestal for a pop-up book. To create more pedestals, students simply make additional pairs of cuts in the folded tag board. These cuts can be made anywhere on the tag board, and they can be as deep and as wide as the students wish to make them. The measurements given above are simply a suggestion.

5. Students select a vocabulary word, write it at the top of their pop-up book, and write a sentence using the vocabulary word at the bottom of their pop-up book.

6. Students decorate the tag board to illustrate the sentence in which the vocabulary word is used. They glue an illustration made out of construction paper on the popped-out pedestal and decorate the rest of the pop-up book to reflect the sentence written at the bottom of the page.

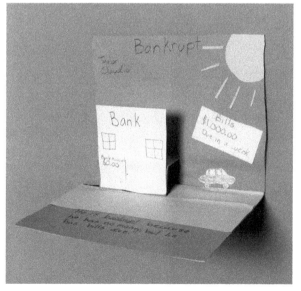

Vocabulary Charades

DESCRIPTION: In this activity, students test their acting skills by acting out the meanings of vocabulary words.

MATERIALS:

- list of vocabulary words

DIRECTIONS:

1. Explain to the students that you will be asking for volunteers to act out vocabulary words. Emphasize that like in the game *charades*, they will only be allowed to act but not speak. They may, however, use props found in the classroom to help their performance.

2. After getting one or two volunteers, provide the student(s) with a vocabulary word and give the student(s) a few minutes to prepare.

3. Provide the rest of the class with the complete list of vocabulary words from which the students will attempt to guess the vocabulary word that is being acted out by their classmate(s).

4. As students raise their hands to guess the word being acted out, allow the actor(s) to call on their classmates to respond.

5. Once the correct answer is given, choose a new student(s) to act out the next word.

Vocabulary Skits

DESCRIPTION: In small groups, students create skits to act out the meaning of vocabulary words and then perform them to the class.

MATERIALS:

- list of vocabulary words

DIRECTIONS:

1. Divide the class into small groups of four to six students, and provide each group with a list of vocabulary words.

2. Explain to the students that their task is to prepare a skit that illustrates the definition of the vocabulary words they select from their list to act out. For example, if their vocabulary word is *vehemently*, the students might create a skit where a child is not at all willing to share his toys with his siblings or friends. Clarify that, unlike in charades, students are allowed to speak while performing their skits. They are not, however, allowed to say the vocabulary word(s) that they are acting out.

3. Allow students approximately five to ten minutes to select one or more vocabulary words to perform and to prepare their skits.

4. After each performance, ask the students in the audience to identify both the vocabulary word that was being acted out and the actions that were used to demonstrate the word. The students in the audience look at their vocabulary list to help them guess the words.

Vocabulary Wheels

DESCRIPTION: Students create a moving wheel that is placed within a folded piece of paper, which has a small opening cut on both sides. Through the small openings, students write vocabulary words on one side of the wheel and their definitions on the other side of the wheel. Students use this visual tool to test vocabulary knowledge.

MATERIALS:

- 1 sheet of construction paper (12" x 18") per student

- 1 circle 9" in diameter made of contrasting colored construction paper per student

- 1 metal brad per student

- markers, crayons, or colored pencils

DIRECTIONS:

1. Provide each student with one 12" x 18" sheet of construction paper and one circle 9" in diameter cut from construction paper.

2. Students fold the sheet of construction paper in half so that the two shorter edges meet.

3. On one side of the folded paper, students measure 2" down from the top center and cut a box 2½" wide and 1½" high. They then cut a matching box on the other side of the paper. These overlapping boxes will be the text boxes of the vocabulary wheel.

4. Students open the folded piece of paper and center the circle on the right half of the sheet of paper. Make sure students leave a ½" leeway between the center fold line and the circle. (When they fold the paper, they will be able to see a part of the circle extend beyond the right edge.) If placed on the fold, the circle will not turn.

5. With a pen or pencil, students poke a hole through the center of the circle and the unfolded construction paper underneath it.

6. Students refold the construction paper and flip it over so that the side with the hole poked through it is facing up. They then poke a pen or pencil through this hole again, through the circle in the middle, and out the other side of the construction paper.

7. Students insert a brad through all three sheets of paper. They now have a vocabulary wheel with corresponding text boxes on both sides.

8. Instruct students to write one vocabulary word in the text box on one side of the wheel and the definition of the word in the text box on the other side of the wheel. Students then turn the wheel until the word and its definition disappear, and write another word and its definition in the corresponding text boxes. Students continue to fill in the wheel with vocabulary words and definitions in this way.

9. Students use this wheel to quiz each other on vocabulary. One student looks at the words written on one side of the wheel and defines them, while the partner looking at the definitions written on the other side of the wheel determines whether the definitions given by her partner are correct.

VARIATION:

Students write prefixes, suffixes, or root words and their definitions in the corresponding text boxes of the vocabulary wheel.

SUGGESTION:

Use the wheel to help students review information in other subjects. For example, students can use it in history class to learn dates, places or other pertinent information and in science class to learn facts about concepts being taught. The vocabulary wheel is an extremely versatile tool and you are encouraged to use it in any way you see fit beyond the uses listed here to help students retain the knowledge that is required of them.

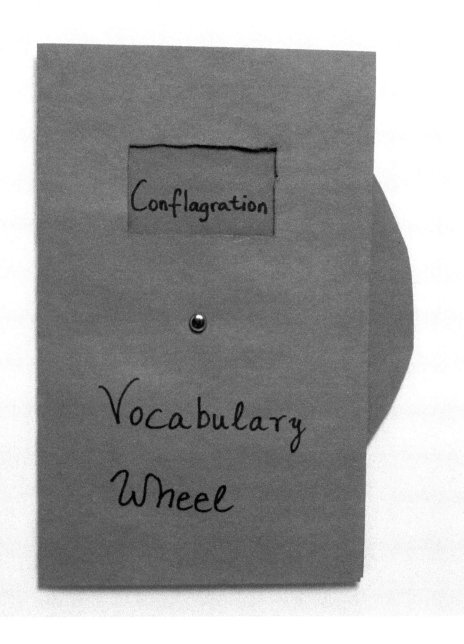

What It Is and What It Isn't

DESCRIPTION: In this activity, students practice their word knowledge by giving examples and non-examples for vocabulary words.

MATERIALS:

- 1 sheet of paper (8½" x 11") per student

- pen or pencil

- list of vocabulary words

DIRECTIONS:

1. Provide each student with one 8½" x 11" sheet of paper and a list of vocabulary words.

2. On a sheet of paper, each student makes three columns, labeling each:

    VOCABULARY WORD **WHAT IT IS** **WHAT IT ISN'T**

3. In the column labeled *Vocabulary Word*, students list their vocabulary words. In the column labeled *What It Is*, students give an example of the corresponding vocabulary word. In the column labeled *What It Isn't*, students give a non-example of the corresponding vocabulary word. See the example below:

    VOCABULARY WORD **WHAT IT IS** **WHAT IT ISN'T**

    ubiquitous   McDonald's   money

4. After several minutes, collect the students' papers. Not all students will have completed giving examples and non-examples for each vocabulary word.

5. From the student responses, randomly call out an example or non-example without revealing the actual vocabulary word. Based on the example or non-example given, students guess the vocabulary word represented by the response. Allow students to use their list of vocabulary words to determine the vocabulary word represented by each example or non-example.

Word Salads

DESCRIPTION: Students create their own word salads made of small squares of construction paper. They 1) write several related words on small squares of green paper to create *lettuce*; 2) pass the *lettuce* to a group mate who determines the relationship between the words and writes it on a red square of paper to create a *tomato*; 3) pass the salad to a third group mate who writes an example of the words on a white square of paper to create an *onion*; and 4) pass the bowl to a fourth person, who writes a non-example for the words on an orange sheet of paper, thus creating a *carrot* and completing the word salad.

MATERIALS:

- 1 paper or styrofoam bowl per student

- 4" squares of construction paper in the following colors:

  - light green (lettuce) – 3 squares per student

  - red (tomato) – 1 square per student

  - white (onion) – 1 square per student

  - orange (carrot) – 1 square per student

- pen or pencil

- scissors

- lists of words that are in some way related to one another

DIRECTIONS:

1. Place students into groups of four.

2. Provide each student with a paper bowl and 4" squares of construction paper in the following colors: light green (3), red (1), white (1), and orange (1). Each student writes his name on the bottom of his bowl.

3. Provide students with lists of vocabulary words from which they choose 5-10 words that are in some way related. For example, the words can all convey an emotion (e.g., happiness, sadness), they can be related to an action (e.g., traveling, playing a sport), or they can express a concept (e.g., ecosystems, civil rights, algebra).

4. Students tear their green squares of paper into strips and write their chosen words on these strips of paper. They then place these pieces in their bowl, creating the *lettuce* for the salad.

5. Each student in a group then passes his bowl to a group member, who reads the *lettuce* and determines the relationship between the words. This student writes the relationship on his square of red construction paper and cuts it to resemble a *tomato* for the salad. He writes his name on the back of his *tomato* and places it in the salad bowl.

6. Each bowl, now containing *lettuce* and a *tomato*, is passed to a third group member. This person reads all the words in the bowl and writes an example for the words on his square of white construction paper, which he then cuts to represent the *onion* of the salad. He writes his name on the back of the onion and adds it to the bowl.

7. Each bowl is passed around a third time to a fourth group member. This student also reads all the words in the salad and writes a non-example for them on his square of orange construction paper. He cuts this paper to resemble a *carrot*, writes his name on the back, and places the paper in the bowl, thus completing the word salad.

8. Each word salad is passed back to the original person whose name appears on the bottom of the bowl. This student checks the relationship, example, and non-example given by his group mates and in cases of discrepancy, discusses the word choice(s) with the appropriate person(s).

9. Once each group has finished, place students into different groups of four to six people.

10. Each student in a group chooses a bowl other than his own, takes out the *tomatoes, onions,* and *carrots,* and places them in a collective pile. Each group mixes its vegetable pile well.

11. Each student reads the words on the *lettuce* left in his bowl, picks out the appropriate *tomato, carrot,* and *onion* from the vegetable pile, and adds them back into his bowl.

SUGGESTION:

This activity can be extended by providing students with the following questionnaire:

Salad Questionnaire

1. Think of another way the words on the lettuce in the salad are related. What is this relationship?_____
   Add another related word (lettuce) to the salad.

2. Write an example for this new relationship._____
   Add another example (onion) to the salad.

3. Write a non-example for this new relationship._____
   Add another non-example (carrot) to the salad.

Word Trees

DESCRIPTION: In small groups, students draw the outline of a tree with many branches. They write one prefix, suffix, or root word in the trunk and then write words that contain this morpheme in the branches of the tree.

MATERIALS:

- list of prefixes, suffixes, and root words (pages 47-50)

- chart paper

- markers: one color for each student in a group

DIRECTIONS:

1. Divide the students into small groups of three or four. Provide each group with one sheet of chart paper and each student in the group with a different colored marker.

2. Instruct each group to draw one large tree with numerous bare branches (no leaves).

3. On the board or overhead projector, provide the class with a list of prefixes, suffixes, and root words. Instruct each group to choose one word from the list and to write it on the trunk of its word tree.

4. Group members write one word containing the main morpheme in each of the branches of their tree. Each member of the group uses a different colored marker to write his word on the word tree.

5. Once all the groups have finished, each group presents its word tree to the class and each group member defines his contributions to the tree.

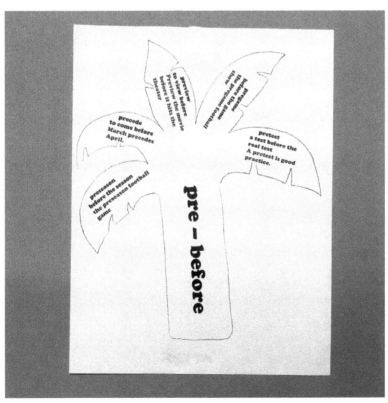

Words in Print

DESCRIPTION: Students look for the vocabulary words they are learning in printed material (e.g., magazines, newspapers) outside of the classroom. They bring the printed material to class, which you photocopy and display on a bulletin board titled *Words in Print*. Use this as an on-going activity that allows students to connect to vocabulary words and understand the different contexts in which these words can be used.

MATERIALS:

- bulletin board

- paper

- pen or pencil

DIRECTIONS:

1. This is an on-going activity that you can have your students do year-round or for as short a time as you prefer. As you teach students new vocabulary words, encourage them to look for these words in printed material (e.g., books, magazines, newspapers) outside of the classroom. Students generally find it exciting to encounter the vocabulary words they are studying outside of the classroom because they not only see that these words are actually being used, they also learn how to use these words correctly.

2. Instruct students to bring to school the materials containing the vocabulary words.

3. Make a copy of the page on which each vocabulary word is located, write the student's name on the photocopy, and hand both the original and the photocopy back to the student.

4. Students then highlight their vocabulary words and, on a separate strip of paper, write the title of the printed material containing the vocabulary words and define the words as they are used in the text. Students attach their strips of paper to the photocopied original text and hand the papers to you.

5. Display each page and definition either on a bulletin board titled *Words in Print* or elsewhere in the classroom.

SUGGESTION:

Provide a treat (e.g., colorful pencil, lollipop) to students for every vocabulary word they locate in print.

More Resources

Common Prefixes

ab- (away from)
abnormal

ante- (before)
antebellum

anti- (against)
antiwar

bi- (two)
biweekly

circum- (around)
circumnavigate

co- (with, together)
coexist

counter- (against)
counterattack

de- (away, down)
depart

dis- (not)
disagree

ex- (from)
ex-president

extra- (outside, beyond)
extraordinary

fore- (in front)
forehead

il- (not)
illegal

im- (not)
impossible

in- (not)
inactive

inter- (between, among)
interplanetary

ir- (not)
irregular

mid- (middle)
midnight

mis- (wrong)
misunderstand

non- (not)
nonsense

post- (after)
postwar

pre- (before)
preheat

pro- (for, before)
pronoun

re- (again)
reword

retro- (backward, back)
retroactive

sub- (under)
submarine

super- (over)
superhuman

trans- (across)
transport

un- (not)
unclear

uni- (one)
unicycle

Common Suffixes

-able, -ible (able to)
enjoyable/compatible

-age (state of being, place of, result of)
orphanage

-al (relating to something)
political

-ance, -ence (state of being)
excellence

-ary, -ery (that which, place where)
bakery

-en (having nature of)
wooden

-en (to make or become)
flatten

-er, -or (person who, state or quality)
baker/actor

-ful (characterized by, full of)
joyful

-fy (make or form into)
simplify

-hood (state of rank)
neighborhood

-ic (pertaining to, like)
athletic

-ion (act, process, state)
education

-ish (having nature of)
childish

-ist (one who)
scientist

-ity, -ty (state of being)
reality

-ive (having nature of, quality of, given to)
active

-ize (to become)
idolize

-less (without)
penniless

-ly (in the manner of)
happily

-ment (resulting state, action or process)
punishment

-ness (quality or state of being)
happiness

-ous (state or condition, having quality of)
humorous

-ship (office, profession, skill)
friendship

-ure (act, process)
failure

Common Root Words

agri (field)
agriculture

anthropo (human)
anthropology

aqua (water)
aquarium

astro (star)
astronomy

audi (hear)
auditorium

auto (self)
autobiography

bio (life)
biology

cardio (heart)
cardiac

cede, ceed, cess (go)
secede

chrom (color)
polychrome

demos (people)
democracy

derma (skin)
epidermis

dict (speak, say, tell)
dictionary

div (separate)
diverse

duct (lead)
conduct

dyna (power)
dynamic

flect (bend)
reflect

geo (earth)
geology

grad (step, stage)
gradual

graph (write, draw)
paragraph

helio (sun)
heliocentric

hydro (water)
hydrology

hypno (sleep)
hypnosis

ject (throw)
eject

magni (great, big)
magnify

man(u) (hand)
manuscript

mono (one)
monochrome

mort (death)
mortal

ortho (straight)
orthodox

phon (sound)
phonetic

photo (light)
photograph

pod (foot)
podiatry

poli (city)
police

port (carry)
airport

psycho (mind)
psychology

pyro (fire)
pyrometer

rupt (break)
disrupt

scope (see)
telescope

script (write)
manuscript

sens, sent (feel)
sensitive

tele (far away)
telephone

terra (earth)
territory

theo (god)
theology

therm (heat)
thermometer

vent (come)
convention

vid, vis (see)
vision

voc (voice, call)
vocal

zoo (animal)
zoology

Additional Root Words

(Use the Blank Card Template on page 68 to create additional root word-definition cards)

acu (sharp)
acute

alter (other)
alternate

ami, amic (love)
amicable

ann, enni (year)
anniversary

arch (chief, leader, ruler)
monarch

bell (war)
belligerent

biblio (book)
bibliography

brev (short)
abbreviate

cap (take, sieze)
captivate

chron (time)
synchronize

cogn (know)
recognize

corp (body)
corporal

cred (believe)
credibility

crypt (hidden)
cryptic

ego (self)
egomania

endo (within)
endoskeleton

equ (equal)
equate

fin (end, ended)
finite

fract, frag (break)
fracture

gen (birth, race, produce)
genetic

holo (whole, entire)
holistic

leg, lect (read, choose)
legible

levi (light)
alleviate

loc (place)
location

magni (great, big)
magnify

medi (half, middle)
mediate

metri, meter (measure)
odometer

migra (wander)
immigrant

mob, mot, mov (move)
promote

morph (form, structure)
amorphous

mut (change)
mutant

neuro (nerve)
neurology

noct, nox (night)
nocturnal

nomen, nomin (name)
nominate

nov (new)
renovate

nym, onym (word, name)
anonymous

pac (peace)
pacifist

pater (father)
patriotic

pot (power)
potent

pugna (fight)
pugnacious

quer, quis (ask)
query

scent, scend (climb)
ascent

sec, sect (cut)
dissect

sed, sess (sit)
sedentary

sol (sun)
solar

tang, tact (touch)
tangible

test (to bear witness)
testimony

tox (poison)
intoxicate

Prefix-Definition Cards

PREFIX	PREFIX	PREFIX
AB-	ANTE-	ANTI-

DEFINITION	DEFINITION	DEFINITION
AWAY FROM	BEFORE	AGAINST

PREFIX	PREFIX	PREFIX
BI-	CIRCUM-	CO-

DEFINITION	DEFINITION	DEFINITION
TWO	AROUND	WITH, TOGETHER

PREFIX	PREFIX	PREFIX
COUNTER-	DE-	DIS-

DEFINITION	DEFINITION	DEFINITION
AGAINST	AWAY, DOWN	NOT

PREFIX	PREFIX	PREFIX
EX-	EXTRA-	FORE-

DEFINITION	DEFINITION	DEFINITION
FROM	OUTSIDE, BEYOND	IN FRONT

PREFIX	PREFIX	PREFIX
IL-	IM-	IN-

DEFINITION	DEFINITION	DEFINITION
NOT	NOT	NOT

PREFIX	PREFIX	PREFIX
INTER-	IR-	MID-

DEFINITION	DEFINITION	DEFINITION
AMONG, BETWEEN	NOT	MIDDLE

PREFIX	PREFIX	PREFIX
MIS-	NON-	POST-

DEFINITION	DEFINITION	DEFINITION
WRONG	NOT	AFTER

PREFIX	PREFIX	PREFIX
PRE-	PRO-	RE-

DEFINITION	DEFINITION	DEFINITION
BEFORE	FOR, BEFORE	AGAIN

PREFIX	PREFIX	PREFIX
RETRO-	SUB-	SUPER-
DEFINITION	DEFINITION	DEFINITION
BACKWARD, BACK	UNDER	OVER
PREFIX	PREFIX	PREFIX
TRANS-	UN-	UNI-
DEFINITION	DEFINITION	DEFINITION
ACROSS	NOT	ONE

Suffix-Definition Cards

SUFFIX	SUFFIX	SUFFIX
-ABLE/-IBLE	-AGE	-AL

DEFINITION	DEFINITION	DEFINITION
ABLE TO	STATE OF BEING, PLACE OF, RESULT OF	RELATING TO SOMETHING

SUFFIX	SUFFIX	SUFFIX
-ANCE/-ENCE	-ARY/-ERY	-EN

DEFINITION	DEFINITION	DEFINITION
STATE OF BEING	THAT WHICH, PLACE WHERE	HAVING NATURE OF, TO MAKE OR BECOME

SUFFIX	SUFFIX	SUFFIX
-ER/-OR	-FUL	-FY
DEFINITION	DEFINITION	DEFINITION
PERSON WHO, STATE OR QUALITY	CHARACTERIZED BY, FULL OF	MAKE OR FORM INTO
SUFFIX	SUFFIX	SUFFIX
-HOOD	-IC	-ION
DEFINITION	DEFINITION	DEFINITION
STATE OF RANK	PERTAINING TO, LIKE	ACT, PROCESS, STATE

SUFFIX	SUFFIX	SUFFIX
-ISH	-IST	-ITY/-TY

DEFINITION	DEFINITION	DEFINITION
HAVING NATURE OF	ONE WHO	STATE OF BEING

SUFFIX	SUFFIX	SUFFIX
-IVE	-IZE	-LESS

DEFINITION	DEFINITION	DEFINITION
HAVING NATURE OF, QUALITY OF, GIVEN TO	TO BECOME	WITHOUT

SUFFIX	SUFFIX	SUFFIX
-LY	-MENT	-NESS

DEFINITION	DEFINITION	DEFINITION
IN THE MANNER OF	RESULTING STATE, ACTION OR PROCESS	QUALITY OR STATE OF BEING

SUFFIX	SUFFIX	SUFFIX
-OUS	-SHIP	-URE

DEFINITION	DEFINITION	DEFINITION
STATE OR CONDITION, HAVING QUALITY OF	OFFICE, SKILL, PROFESSION	ACT, PROCESS

Root Word-Definition Cards

ROOT WORD	ROOT WORD	ROOT WORD
AGRI	ANTHROPO	AQUA

DEFINITION	DEFINITION	DEFINITION
FIELD	HUMAN	WATER

ROOT WORD	ROOT WORD	ROOT WORD
ASTRO	AUDI	AUTO

DEFINITION	DEFINITION	DEFINITION
STAR	HEAR	SELF

ROOT WORD	ROOT WORD	ROOT WORD
BIO	CARDIO	CEDE, CEED, CESS
DEFINITION	DEFINITION	DEFINITION
LIFE	HEART	GO
ROOT WORD	ROOT WORD	ROOT WORD
CHROM	DEMOS	DERMA
DEFINITION	DEFINITION	DEFINITION
COLOR	PEOPLE	SKIN

ROOT WORD	ROOT WORD	ROOT WORD
DICT	DIV	DUCT

DEFINITION	DEFINITION	DEFINITION
SPEAK, SAY, TELL	SEPARATE	LEAD

ROOT WORD	ROOT WORD	ROOT WORD
DYNA	FLECT	GEO

DEFINITION	DEFINITION	DEFINITION
POWER	BEND	EARTH

ROOT WORD	ROOT WORD	ROOT WORD
GRAD	GRAPH	HELIO

DEFINITION	DEFINITION	DEFINITION
STEP, STAGE	WRITE, DRAW	SUN

ROOT WORD	ROOT WORD	ROOT WORD
HYDRO	HYPNO	JECT

DEFINITION	DEFINITION	DEFINITION
WATER	SLEEP	THROW

ROOT WORD	ROOT WORD	ROOT WORD
MAGNI	MAN(U)	MONO

DEFINITION	DEFINITION	DEFINITION
GREAT, BIG	HAND	ONE

ROOT WORD	ROOT WORD	ROOT WORD
MORT	ORTHO	PHON

DEFINITION	DEFINITION	DEFINITION
DEATH	STRAIGHT	SOUND

ROOT WORD	ROOT WORD	ROOT WORD
PHOTO	POD	POLI

DEFINITION	DEFINITION	DEFINITION
LIGHT	FOOT	CITY

ROOT WORD	ROOT WORD	ROOT WORD
PORT	PSYCHO	PYRO

DEFINITION	DEFINITION	DEFINITION
CARRY	MIND	FIRE

ROOT WORD	ROOT WORD	ROOT WORD
RUPT	SCOPE	SCRIPT

DEFINITION	DEFINITION	DEFINITION
BREAK	SEE	WRITE

ROOT WORD	ROOT WORD	ROOT WORD
SENS, SENT	TELE	TERRA

DEFINITION	DEFINITION	DEFINITION
FEEL	FAR AWAY	EARTH

ROOT WORD	ROOT WORD	ROOT WORD
THEO	THERM	VENT
DEFINITION	**DEFINITION**	**DEFINITION**
GOD	HEAT	COME
ROOT WORD	ROOT WORD	ROOT WORD
VID, VIS	VOC	ZOO
DEFINITION	**DEFINITION**	**DEFINITION**
SEE	VOICE, CALL	ANIMAL

Blank Card Template

WORD	WORD	WORD
DEFINITION	DEFINITION	DEFINITION
WORD	WORD	WORD
DEFINITION	DEFINITION	DEFINITION

Cross-index of Games and Activities

Bibliography

Bear, D.R., Invernizzi, M., Templeton, S., and Johnston, F. (2004). *Words their way: Word study for phonics, vocabulary, and spelling instruction.* Upper Saddle River, NJ: Pearson/Merrill Prentice Hall.

Beck, I.L., McKeown, M.G., and Kucan, L. (2002). *Bringing words to life: Robust vocabulary instruction.* NY, NY: Guilford Press.

Blachowicz, C. and Fisher, P.J. (2006). *Teaching vocabulary in all classrooms.* Upper Saddle River, NJ: Pearson/Merrill Prentice Hall.

Blachowicz, C., Fisher, P.J., Ogle, D., and Watts-Taffe, S. (2006). Theory and research into practice: Vocabulary questions from the classroom. *Reading Research Quarterly (IRA).* 41(4), 525-535.

Graves, M.F. (2006). *The vocabulary book: Learning and instruction.* New York: Teachers College Press.

Kieffer, M.J. and Lesaux, N.K. (2007). Breaking down words to build meaning: Morphology, vocabulary, and reading comprehension in the urban classroom. *The Reading Teacher.* 61(2), 134-144.

Lavoie, R.D. (1989). *Understanding Learning Disabilities – How Difficult Can It Be?* Modified from *F.A.T. City Workshop,* PBS Video. Alexandria, VA: Greater Washington Educational Telecommunication Association, Inc.

National Reading Panel. (2000). *Teaching children to read: An evidence-based assessment of the scientific research literature on reading and its implications for reading instruction.* Washington, DC: National Institute for Literacy and The Partnership for Reading.

Tompkins, G.E. and Blanchfield, C. (2004). *Teaching vocabulary: 50 creative strategies, grades K–12.* Upper Saddle River, NJ: Pearson/Merrill Prentice Hall.

Yopp, R.H. and Yopp, H.K. (2007). The important words plus: A strategy for building word knowledge. *The Reading Teacher.* 61(2), 157-160.